home & garden
metalcrafts

jana ewy

NORTH LIGHT BOOKS
Cincinnati, Ohio
www.artistsnetwork.com

metric conversion chart

TO CONVERT	TO	MULTIPLY BY
Inches	Centimeters	2.54
Centimeters	Inches	0.4
Feet	Centimeters	30.5
Centimeters	Feet	0.03
Yards	Meters	0.9
Meters	Yards	1.1
Sq. Inches	Sq. Centimeters	6.45
Sq. Centimeters	Sq. Inches	0.16
Sq. Feet	Sq. Meters	0.09
Sq. Meters	Sq. Feet	10.8
Sq. Yards	Sq. Meters	0.8
Sq. Meters	Sq. Yards	1.2
Pounds	Kilograms	0.45
Kilograms	Pounds	2.2
Ounces	Grams	28.4
Grams	Ounces	0.04

Home & Garden Metalcrafts. © 2002 by Jana Ewy. Manufactured in China. All rights reserved. The patterns in this book are for the personal use of the reader. By permission of the author and the publisher, they may be either hand traced or photocopied to make single copies, but under no circumstances may they be resold or republished. No other part of this book may be reproduced in any form or by any electronic or mechanical means, including information storage and retrieval systems, without permission in writing from the publisher, except by a reviewer, who may quote brief passages in a review. Published by North Light Books, an imprint of F&W Publications, Inc., 4700 East Galbraith Road, Cincinnati, Ohio 45236. (800) 289-0963. First edition.

Other fine North Light Books are available from your local bookstore, art supply store or direct from the publisher.

06 05 04 03 02   5 4 3 2 1

Library of Congress Cataloging-in-Publication Data

Ewy, Jana
    Home & garden metalcrafts / by Jana Ewy. — 1st ed.
            p. cm.
    Includes index.
    ISBN 1-58180-330-3 (pbk. : alk. paper)
     1. Metal-work. 2. House furnishings. 3. Garden ornaments and furniture. I. Title:
    Home and garden metalcrafts. II. Title.
    TT213 .E98 2003
    684.1'05 — dc21

2002075159

Editor: Liz Koffel Schneiders
Designer: Andrea Short
Production coordinator: Sara Dumford
Production artist: Kathy Bergstrom
Photography: Tim Grondin
Photo Stylist: Jan Nickum

about the author

As a designer, Jana Ewy is always aspiring to reach a new level of creativity. As a demonstrator and teacher, she obtains the greatest pleasures from sharing her love for crafting with all who she meets. As a product developer, which is new to Jana, she is grateful for the opportunity to create and develop effective and useful tools for crafters to work with.

Jana is a member of the Society of Craft Designers. She contributes to many popular craft magazines, has written several how-to books, and appears as a guest on television shows demonstrating all kinds of craft techniques. Above all, Jana is proud to be the wife of her wonderful husband, Mike; and the mother to three terrific sons; Greg, Adam and Dustin.

acknowledgments

Many thanks to my family and friends, who have given me such wonderful support, encouragement and inspiration. To the many manufacturers, who have given so generously of their wonderful products. To Mark Lee and the incredible AMACO family, for believing in me and giving me the opportunity to express my creativity and share it with so many. To the staff at North Light Books, whose warmth and kindness made the process of writing this book a pure pleasure. You have my admiration for producing such a quality product.

table of contents

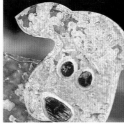

projects:

introduction

● ● ● Accents make your home and garden more personal and inviting. Currently, the use of metal seems to be a big standout in home decor. There is an incredible array of exciting techniques, from rustic to elegant, that are popping up everywhere. Even if you have never worked with metal before, you will want to give it a try. Luckily, there is now a wonderful assortment of crafting metals and meshes available at your local craft retailers. And the tools needed to work with these metals are basic craft tools that you probably already have at home.

● ● ● As you know, buying something never gives the pleasure that making something does. With that in mind, I hope you'll find one or more of these projects inspiring enough for you to give metal crafting a try. All of the projects are fun and easy to complete. The detailed step-by-step instructions show you how to create not only practical but exotic and magical accessories for both your home and your garden. Enjoy your creative journey!

– jana ewy

Materials & Tools

Here are all the materials and tools you will need to complete the projects in this book. You can find most of these project materials and tools, plus an assortment of craft metal, wire and mesh, at most craft retailers. Check out your local hardware store for any additional materials and basic tools.

Metals & Meshes

Embossing Metal

Embossing metal sheets come in a variety of weights and finishes: copper, aluminum, brass, pewter and colored aluminum. The copper, aluminum, brass and pewter metals come in 9¼" x 12" (24cm x 30.5cm) rolls. The colored aluminum comes in a variety of colorful shades and is packaged in rolls of 9¼" x 5' (24cm x 1.5m). Embossing metals also come in two weights: light and medium. All of the projects in this book use medium-weight metal.

Aluminum, copper and brass mesh come in several mesh counts. Embossing metal of light or medium thickness is sold in rolls.

Wire Mesh

Wire mesh is a woven wire cloth. Like embossing metal, it comes in various metals, such as copper and brass. The different-sized weaves are measured by the gauge (the thickness of the wire) and the mesh count, or number of wires to the inch (2.5cm). For example, if a project calls for copper 8 mesh, you will use a coarse mesh with only eight wires to the inch (2.5cm). Copper 80 mesh is a very fine mesh that looks more like cloth. Meshes can be found in craft stores packaged as flat sheets, folded sheets or in rolls.

Wire

Wire is available in many colors and thicknesses. It is measured by gauge numbers. As the wire's diameter increases, the gauge number gets smaller. Different projects require different types of wires and different gauges. Wire is also available with a plastic coating, which is great for outdoor projects. Most wire comes coiled or on spools.

Armature Rods

Armature rods are thick rods that come in a variety of metals. Their thickness is measured by fractions of an inch or millimeters. Harder metals, such as copper and brass, come in straight rods that are good for plant stakes. Softer aluminum rods can be found in coils and are good for projects that require bending or coiling.

Copper Tubing and Pipe

Copper tubing and copper pipe are inexpensive and easily found at your local hardware or home improvement store. Copper tubing is measured in fractions of an inch (in millimeters) and comes in large coils of various lengths. It can be cut with a pipe cutter. Copper pipe and copper pipe fittings are found in the plumbing department. Pipe comes in various diameters measured by the inch or millimeter. Most hardware stores will cut pipe to size for you, or you can cut it yourself with a pipe cutter.

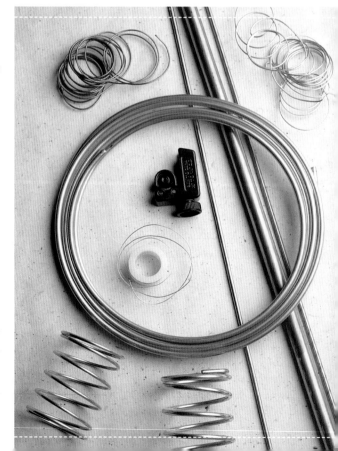

Fine gauge craft wire, both plain and plastic-coated is perfect for small projects and embellishments. Straight aluminum armature rods make good supports and plant stakes. Copper tubing and pipe can be cut with a pipe cutter and used in larger metal craft projects.

A strong heat gun and cookie sheet are all you need for heating metal. A drill is useful for mounting wire in a wood base. A rubber mallet with a textured head makes distressing metal easy. Set grommets with a hammer and smooth out any rough spots with a brayer. Finally, a sheet of craft foam is a good cushion when texturing metal.

●●● Tools

Heat Gun

Heat guns are wonderful for heating copper metal and mesh in order to change the color. Choose a heat gun with a focused, more intense airflow for the best results.

Baking Sheet

A metal baking sheet is used when heating the copper metal and mesh. Not only does it act as a protective barrier so your project does not blow away, it helps to contain the heat so the process works a little faster.

Rubber Mallet

This is the metal-crafting tool that I can't live without. By adding beads of hot glue to one end, you have a wonderful texturing tool. Turn to page 12 to learn how to make your own textured mallet. Use sheets of craft foam to provide a good cushion under metal sheets when embossing and texturing.

Brayer

A brayer is helpful for smoothing and flattening metals and meshes after they have been textured.

Hammer

A hammer is used for attaching grommets.

Drill

Besides being used to drill holes in wood beads, it's a great tool for twisting wires.

Cutting Mat

A good quality self-healing mat with an easy-to-read grid will help make all your measuring and cutting jobs easier.

Ruler

A clear quilter's ruler the size of your cutting mat allows you to measure and cut large or small jobs accurately. You will find the marked measurement lines on the ruler very helpful.

Rotary Cutter

For straight, perfect cuts every time, rotary cutters slice through embossing metals and fine-gauge wire mesh fabric with ease. It's fast and easy.

Grommet Tool

This two-part tool, along with a hammer, is used for setting grommets. Each size grommet requires a setting tool of the same size.

Wire Cutters

Wire cutters are used to cut heavier gauge wire and armature rods.

Scissors

A good pair of sharp scissors makes cutting out curved metal shapes a breeze. They are also good for cutting through meshes and lightweight wire. You may want to have at least two pairs just for metal crafting.

Decorative Scissors and Punches

Decorative-edge scissors and decorative punches can also be used to cut metal and wire mesh fabric.

Pliers

Round-nose jewelry pliers are used to manipulate wire and rods into creative shapes like spirals and loops. Needle-nose pliers can be used to grip and crimp (squeeze closed) wires and jump rings.

Hole Punches

Hand-gripped hole punches in several sizes, $\frac{1}{16}$", $\frac{1}{8}$" and $\frac{1}{4}$" (1.5mm, 3mm and 6mm) are useful for making holes in metal for charms, wires, grommets and beads.

Embossing Tools

Embossing styluses come in two sizes: fine- and medium-point. They are used to trace templates, emboss details in patterns and score fold lines. The contoured embossing tool is used to fill out larger embossing details. The needle tool is used to add a tin-punch detail to projects. It can also be used in place of a $\frac{1}{16}$" (1.5mm) hole punch.

Clockwise from the top: A $\frac{1}{16}$" (1.5mm) hole punch, scissors, needle tool, wooden dowel, a set of three embossing tools, decorative edging scissors, needle-nose pliers, a $\frac{1}{8}$" (3mm) hole punch, round-nose pliers, a $\frac{1}{4}$" hole punch, rotary cutter and wire cutters. In the center: $\frac{1}{4}$" (6mm) brass grommets and a grommet setting tool. A clear quilt ruler and large cutting mat finish the list of useful supplies.

●●● Miscellaneous Supplies

Permanent Markers

These work best to trace templates onto the wire mesh fabric. Just remember to cut inside the tracing line, so none of the markings show.

Cleaning Solutions

Acetone or nail polish remover can be used to clean oils and fingerprints from brass, copper and aluminum. My favorite use, (described on page 15), is to remove the color-coated finish applied to the colored aluminum metals.

Acrylic Paint

Acrylic paint can be used to add accent color where needed. Keep in mind that a clear sealant needs to be applied over it for protection.

Rub 'n Buff

Rub 'n Buff comes in a variety of matte and metallic finishes. This wax-based paste becomes permanent when dry. Like its name implies, the color is rubbed on, allowed to dry, and then buffed to a sheen. I like to use it to add color to metal when creating distressed and aged finishes.

Patina Solutions

Patina solutions like Sophisticated Finishes give copper and brass a beautiful and natural blue or green weathered finish.

Spray Paint

Krylon metallic spray paints are a perfect color match to the actual color of metals.

Beads

Beads are the perfect embellishment to so many projects. They add color, texture and movement.

Spray Adhesive

3M's Super 77 spray adhesive is perfect for quick and permanent adhesion with lighter-weight aluminum metals. You do have to make sure your positioning and placement is correct. Repositioning is usually not an option.

Craft Glue

E6000 craft glue is at the top of my list when it comes to working with metals. It doesn't run or drip, and it won't rust the metals. It is a clear, industrial-strength adhesive that is waterproof and flexible.

Clockwise from the top: metal and glass paint, Rub n' Buff, industrial-strength craft adhesive, a hot glue gun, antique patina solution, metallic spray paints, spray adhesive, acrylic paint, permanent marker and nail polish remover. Center: assorted seed beads, heavy-duty double-stick tape and a decorative punch.

Double-Stick Tape

For the projects in this book, I recommend using Ultimate Bond, a heavy-duty tape which comes in 9" x 12" (23cm x 31cm) sheets and in rolls of varying widths. It is clean, quick and easy to use. Unlike ordinary, light-weight double-stick tape, Ultimate Bond becomes permanent. It can tolerate heat and cold without losing its adhesion. It's great for heavier-weight metals like copper, brass and pewter.

Glue Guns and Glue Sticks

Glue guns and hot glue sticks are not compatible with metal. However, you will need one to create the textured rubber mallet on page 12 that is used in many of the projects found here.

Basic Techniques

If you haven't worked with metal and wire before, I recommend you take a moment to read through the basic techniques described in this section. One thing you'll notice about many of the projects in this book is that the metal and mesh is rarely used without altering it in some interesting way. These demonstrations will help teach you how to get the best results when you texture and emboss metal, color metal and mesh with a heat gun, and twist, cut and curl wire. These tips will make your projects a success from the very start. Once you're feeling adventurous, try experimenting with variations on these techniques. You may find, as I have, that there's no end to the pleasures of metalcrafting.

safety first!

Wear gloves if you are working with sharp edges or strong paints, adhesives or solutions. Always read the directions provided by the manufacturer. Wait until metal has completely cooled after you have colored it with a heat gun. Practice these general precautions, and you will find that metal and wire are quite easy to work with and offer a surprising range of creative possibilities.

● ● ● Creating a Textured Rubber Mallet

Several of the projects in this book will ask you to use a textured mallet. When I first created this mallet, I had no idea it would become my most treasured metal-crafting tool. When I hammered on that first piece of metal, it was love at first sight. I was able to create a soft hammered look, like that of a professional metalsmith. It is fast, easy and perfect every time. Very few metal projects pass through my hands that don't get some creative texturing.

The following page describes two different ways you can use your custom mallet to texture metal. I'm sure you'll enjoy them both and will want to come up with your own projects to show off these marvelous effects.

Use alcohol or acetone to clean and remove any oils from one of the heads of a rubber mallet. Apply pea-sized beads of hot glue to the head. Start at the edge and work toward the center. It's OK if some of the beads meld together or are slightly different sizes. Let the glue dry.

NOTE: If beads of glue come off at any time, just reattach them with heavy-duty double-stick tape.

[Textured-Mallet Technique One] • Creating a Soft Hammered Look

Add a little bit of sparkle to any metallic surface with this fast and easy technique.

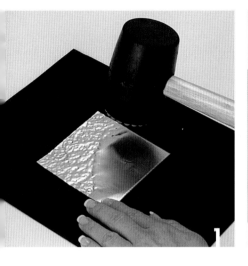
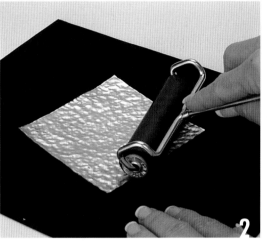
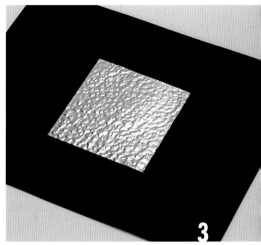

one: Place the metal you wish to texture onto a sheet of craft foam to cushion it and gently hammer it with your textured mallet.

two: If the metal becomes a little misshapen, brayer over it to flatten it down.

three: Flip your metal sheet over to see the final effect. Depending on the project, you may choose whichever side looks best when you use this technique.

[Textured-Mallet Technique Two] • Creating Texture with a Woven Pattern

This technique takes the soft hammered look above one step further. The result is a wonderful surface with a delicate woven effect.

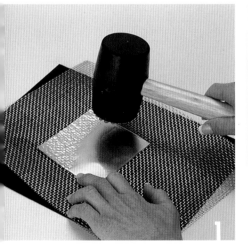

one: Place a piece of metal 8 mesh onto a sheet of craft foam to cushion it. Place the metal on top of the screen and hammer it with your textured mallet.

two: Remove the screen and brayer over the textured metal to flatten it.

three: Flip your sheet over to see the final effect. You may want to experiment with different mesh counts to find one you like the best.

Heating Copper to Change its Color

It is exciting and amazing to watch as heat from a simple heat gun can change a plain sheet of copper into a rainbow of colors. Choose a heat gun with a hot, concentrated airflow. The sequence in which the color changes is always the same. Knowing this, you can determine the color you want and create a variety of patterns or designs.

Changing Color on Copper Metal

Place the copper on a baking sheet. Apply heat to one corner only and watch as the color begins to change to orange, rust, maroon, bluish-purple and then gold. Gold is the final color; once it has been reached, you should move to another area.

Making Straight Lines of Color

Place the metal foil or mesh on a baking sheet. Apply heat, starting at the corner. As the color begins to change, slowly move the heat gun just along the edge. Try to keep a steady hand with even movement.

When heating copper mesh, if you prop it against the edge of the baking sheet and allow the air to flow through it, the color change will be faster and more even.

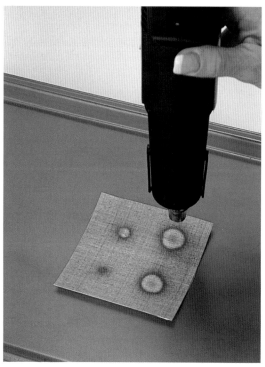

Adding Dots of Color

Place the mesh on a baking sheet. Holding the heat gun directly over the mesh, direct the flow of air at the desired spot. Hold still as the color begins to change. The longer you hold that position, the larger the dot will become. As soon as the desired size is achieved, lift the gun and move to another spot. Repeat as desired.

●●● Distressing Metal

Try this technique any time you are working with colored aluminum metals. By rubbing acetone over a wrinkled metal surface, you reveal bright silver-colored highlights from the aluminum that lies underneath. Add a bit of Rub 'n Buff first, and you'll create a metal surface as exotic as a wild animal skin.

one: Carefully crumple the first sheet of aluminum embossing metal. You should wear gloves to protect your hands from being cut. Pull from the sides of the metal to reshape and slightly flatten it.

two: Apply black Rub 'n Buff with a cloth or paper towel to the gold side of the sheet. Continue to rub until you see some of the metallic surface begin to appear. The metal will continue to flatten as you apply pressure while rubbing. Set the sheet aside to dry.

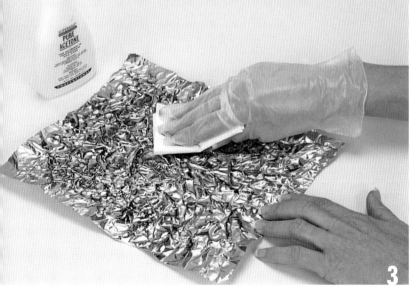

three: Apply acetone to a cloth and lightly rub over the metal to expose some of the silver highlights.

four: Lay the metal sheet on a flat surface and use a brayer to flatten it out completely.

●●• Embossing Metal

A good set of embossing tools is indispensable when working with metal. With a couple of pointed and curved embossing styluses, you can trace patterns, add texture and create depth in your pieces. With a needle tool, you can create a decorative tin-punch border. Here are the most important techniques to learn for adding pizazz to your projects.

Tracing With a Stylus

This technique is good for tracing all of the templates in this book and adding details to a basic pattern. Place your metal sheet onto a sheet of craft foam or other soft surface to cushion it. Lightly trace over your pattern with a fine-point stylus to transfer it onto the metal.

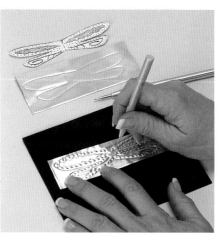

Creating a Tin-Punch Effect

A tin-punch design can be easily made by piercing through metal with a needle tool. Cushion your work on a sheet of craft foam. A needle tool is also good for punching small holes used to hang embellishments like beads and charms with wire or thread.

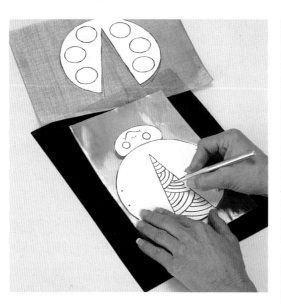

Adding Texture With Embossing Tools

You can add texture to a small area by tapping the surface of the metal with a medium-point stylus. Cushion the metal on a sheet of craft foam for the best results.

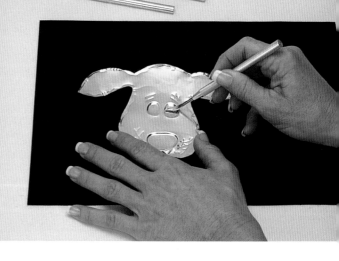

Adding Dimension With a Curved Stylus

For a "puffy," embossed design, flip the metal you want to emboss over on a foam sheet. Retrace the lines of your pattern several times. To achieve depth in large areas, puff them out with a contour stylus, blending tool or even a pencil eraser.

●●● Working With Wire

There are so many fun things you can do with wire. With a few basic tools you can twist, spiral or coil it into creative shapes or quickly create your own jump rings. Experiment with wire in all different gauges and colors to achieve just the look you want for your metalcraft projects.

Twisting Wire

Take a desired length of wire and fold it in half around a dowel. Insert the ends of the wire into the chuck of an electric drill and tighten to secure. Hold the dowel secure in one hand and slowly squeeze the trigger of the drill with the other. Watch as you create the perfect twist.

Making a Spiral

Grip the end of the wire with a pair of round nose pliers and twist to form a small loop. Hold the loop with the pliers and continue to twist the remaining length of wire around it, forming a spiral. Hold the remaining wire between your thumb and forefinger for control.

Making a Coil

Using your thumb or forefinger to brace the wire against a dowel, wind the wire around the dowel until you have a tight, even coil. Gradually slide your thumb or finger along the dowel as the coil lengthens. To remove, simply slide the coil off.

Making Jump Rings

You can buy jump rings, but they are also easy to make. Create a coil with wire. If you need eight jump rings, you need to wrap the wire around a dowel eight times. Trim the ends of the wire as close as possible to the dowel. Slide the coiled wire off. With a small pair of sharp scissors, cut through the loops of the coil.

mesh candleholders

These charming little candleholders are so easy to make you could assemble a dozen in a single afternoon. The luster of fine copper is enhanced by both texturing and heating the mesh—two techniques you will absolutely love! Trimmed with bows and a handful of stars, these candleholders will add instant sparkle to your fireplace mantle, dining room table or bedroom nightstand. Change the color of the bows to coordinate with your favorite decorations, and these candleholders will hold their appeal year-round.

[checklist] • materials & tools

☐ sheet copper 80 metal mesh   ☐ sheet of copper 8 metal mesh   ☐ sheet of craft foam   ☐ 2" (5cm) diameter clear plastic tube with one end closed, cut 6" (15cm) tall (You can use the tube the embossing metal comes in.)   ☐ $\frac{1}{4}$" (6mm) wide heavy-duty double-stick tape

☐ sheet of light copper embossing metal   ☐ 12" (30.5cm) of 24-gauge copper wire   ☐ tea light candle   ☐ baking sheet   ☐ heat gun

☐ textured rubber mallet (See page 12 for instructions on how to make one.)   ☐ 12" (30.5cm) of 1" (2.5cm) wide sheer wired ribbon

☐ brayer   ☐ $\frac{1}{16}$" (1.5mm) hole punch or awl   ☐ star-shaped paper punch   ☐ round-nose pliers

two: Place a piece of copper 8 mesh over some craft foam to cushion it. Place the copper 80 mesh fabric on top and hammer it with a textured mallet. (See page 13 for basic techniques.) This will create an interesting surface on your candleholder. Brayer over the mesh to smooth it out.

one: With a pair of scissors, cut the sheet of copper 80 mesh fabric to 6" x 6½" (15cm x 16.5cm). Place the mesh on a baking sheet and heat three of the four edges with your heat gun until they change color. Leave one short edge undone. Let the mesh cool.

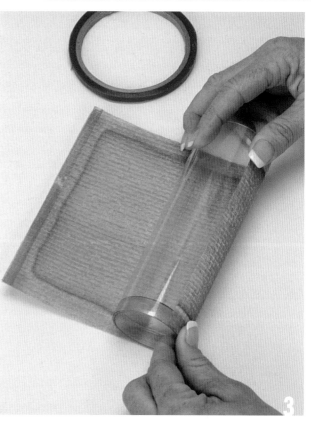

three: Place a strip of heavy-duty double-stick tape along both of the 6" (15cm) sides. Remove the tape backing. Align and stick the unheated edge of the mesh to the tube. Roll the mesh around the tube and secure the opposite edge by pressing along the tape line.

four: Cut and texture with your mallet a 2" x 4" (5cm x 10cm) piece of light copper embossing metal. Punch out two stars with the star punch. Use a $\frac{1}{16}$" (1.5mm) hole punch or awl to punch a hole in each star. Coil the 12" (30.5cm) length of wire around a pencil. Form a loop at each end with round-nose pliers and attach the stars.

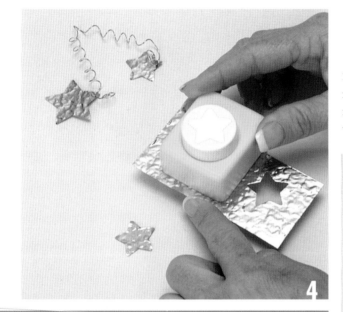

five: Tie a knot around the center of the wire with some ribbon. Place the closed end of the tube facing up. Wrap the ribbon around the candleholder and tie in back, tucking in the loose ends.

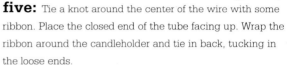

finished candleholders • • • •

six: Place a tea light in the top of your candleholder. Try making several candleholders of different heights. Make your next dinner special by clustering them together for an interesting centerpiece or setting one at each place setting.

metallic picture frame

Featuring a stylish animal print, this picture frame is an extraordinary accent in any room. The distressing technique used to create its unusual surface is simply amazing. You would never guess that behind the decorative metal cover, it is nothing more than a simple Lucite frame! You will be surprised by how easy this project is to make, and you can modify the design to accommodate any size photo or frame.

[checklist] • materials & tools

☐ two sheets of 9¼" x 11" (24cm x 28cm) medium-weight gold aluminum embossing metal (gold on one side and silver on other)   ☐ black Rub 'n Buff

☐ soft cloth or paper towels   ☐ acetone (nail polish remover)   ☐ sheet of craft foam   ☐ spray adhesive   ☐ ½" (1cm) heavy-duty double-stick tape

☐ 8" x 10" (20.5cm x 25.5cm) free-standing Lucite picture frame   ☐ plastic gloves   ☐ brayer   ☐ rotary cutter   ☐ cutting mat   ☐ craft knife

☐ large quilting ruler   ☐ fine-point stylus   ☐ textured rubber mallet (See page 12 for instructions on how to make one.)

one: Carefully crumple the first sheet of aluminum embossing metal. You should wear gloves to protect your hands from being cut. Pull from the sides of the metal to reshape and slightly flatten it.

two: Apply black Rub 'n Duff with a cloth or paper towel to the gold side of the sheet. Continue to rub until you see some of the metallic surface begin to appear. The metal will continue to flatten as you apply pressure while rubbing. Set the sheet aside to dry.

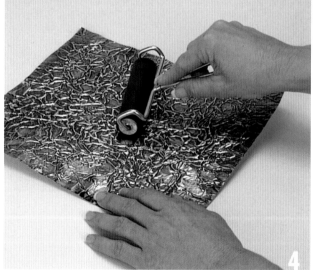

three: Apply acetone to a cloth and lightly rub over the metal to expose some of the silver highlights.

four: Lay the metal sheet on a flat surface and use a brayer to flatten it out completely.

five: Place the second sheet of gold aluminum embossing metal on the craft foam and texture it with your textured rubber mallet.

six: Carefully coat the gold side of this metal sheet with spray adhesive. Follow the directions on the can.

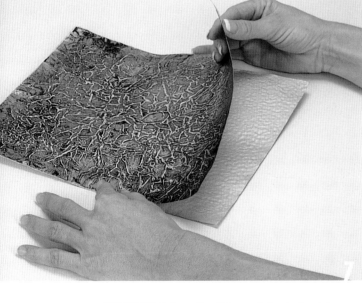

seven: Adhere the distressed sheet of metal over the textured sheet. Brayer over both metal sheets using a light pressure to secure the bond.

eight: Trim the metal sheet with a rotary cutter to 8" x 10" (20.5cm x 25.5cm). Based on the size of your picture, determine the size of the frame opening. I chose to have a 1½" (4cm) border on all four sides, which is perfect for a 5" x 7" (12.5cm x 18cm) photo. Measure and use a stylus to score where the frame opening will be.

nine: Using the score lines as your guide, cut an "X" in the center opening. For this cut, use a craft knife and ruler instead of your rotary cutter.

ten: Flip the sheet silver side up and apply strips of heavy-duty double-stick tape around the outside border and the center opening. Remove the backing from the tape.

tip

For smaller photos, use decorative paper to create a mat frame for a more dramatic look. Coordinate the paper with the colors in the metal sheet and the photograph.

eleven: Carefully position the metal frame over the Lucite frame and gently press into place.

twelve: Curl open each of the flaps to finish your picture frame.

•••• finished picture frame

thirteen: Place a picture of that special someone inside your frame and proudly display it on your desk or dresser. The Lucite frame is great for protecting your photos. The contrasting textures and colors of the metal will make this a technique you will want to use again and again.

fringed lamp

Embellishing miniature lamps is a great way to express your creativity, and this lamp is the ideal project when you want to take a walk on the wild side. Here, you'll discover how textured metal foils can transform a basic shade into something eye-catching. This lamp's exotic appearance and decorative fringe will bring a touch of the jungle to your tamest desktop or bookshelf. If you want to take the effect even further, top off your lamp with a few black feathers and pair it with the **Wild Trinket Box** on page 33.

- -

[checklist] • materials & tools

☐ 6" (15cm) diameter mini lamp shade   ☐ 11" x 14" (28cm x 36cm) piece of scrap paper (for the **lamp-shade pattern**)   ☐ 9¼" x 12" (24cm x 31cm) sheet of medium-weight gold aluminum embossing metal   ☐ soft cloth or paper towels   ☐ black Rub 'n Buff   ☐ acetone (nail polish remover)   ☐ spray adhesive   ☐ ¼" (6mm) wide heavy-duty double-stick tape   ☐ black decorative fringe   ☐ 7" (18cm) tall brass candleholder   ☐ silver spray paint   ☐ candle lamp with batteries (or an electric one)   ☐ zebra-print gift wrap or origami paper   ☐ industrial-strength craft glue   ☐ plastic gloves   ☐ brayer   ☐ fine-point embossing stylus   ☐ scissors

fringed lamp

one: Begin by making a lamp-shade pattern. Using the shade's seam as your starting point, place your shade on the upper left edge of your scrap paper. Slowly roll and mark along both the top and bottom edges of the shade. Continue marking until you reach the seam again and add ½" (1.5cm) for overlap. Cut out your pattern.

two: Texture and distress the gold aluminum metal by following the steps on page 15. Trace your pattern onto the metal sheet with a stylus and use scissors to cut it out.

three: Coat the back of the metal with spray adhesive. Adhere it to the shade, carefully lining up the top and bottom edges.

four: Apply a strip of heavy-duty double-stick tape to the inside bottom edge of the shade and remove the tape backing. Adhere the decorative fringe to the tape strip, trimming any excess. If you prefer, you can also use hot glue for this step.

six: Take the candle out of its plastic base. Measure and cut the zebra-print paper to the size needed to wrap around the candle. Use double-stick tape or spray adhesive to adhere the paper to the candle.

five: Spray the brass candleholder with silver spray paint and let it dry.

•••• finished fringed lamp

seven: Glue the candle into the silver candleholder and add the lamp shade. Since this lamp is battery operated, you can add a soft glow of light just about anywhere. No need to worry about cords and plugs!

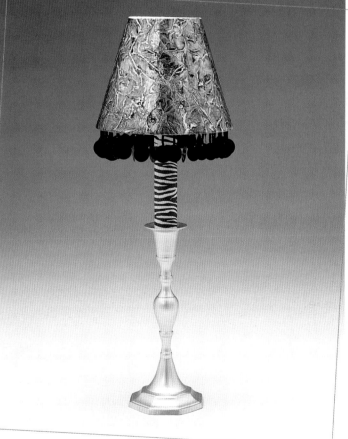

wild trinket box

This safari-style trinket box can be used to stash away your loose change, jewelry, paper clips or anything else you wish to get off your desk. It also makes a wonderful decorative statement when paired with the Fringed Lamp on page 29. The black feathers add just the right amount of whimsy. Why not make two and give one to a friend?

[checklist] • materials & tools

□ 6" x 6" (15cm x 15cm) sheet of medium-weight gold aluminum embossing metal (adjust the dimensions, depending on your box size)

□ black Rub 'n Buff   □ acetone (nail polish remover)   □ soft cloth or paper towel   □ 4" x 4" x 2" (10cm x 10cm x 5cm) papier mâché box

□ scrap paper (for box-lid template)   □ wooden doll-head bead, 2" (5cm) in diameter   □ black acrylic paint   □ zebra-print decorative paper

(wrapping or origami paper)   □ four wooden doll-head beads, 1½" (4cm) in diameter   □ spray adhesive   □ silver spray paint   □ brayer

□ industrial-strength craft glue   □ black feathers   □ plastic gloves   □ fine-point embossing stylus   □ ruler   □ scissors   □ drill and ⅛"

(3mm) drill bit   □ 1" (2.5cm) wide foam brush

one: Texture and distress the gold aluminum metal sheet by following the steps on page 15. Measure the top and sides of the box lid and draw them on scrap paper to create a template. Add ⅜" (1cm) to all four sides; this will allow you to fold the metal over the edge of the lid. Cut out the template, trace it onto the metal with a stylus and score the fold lines. Cut the traced pattern out and cut around the corner tabs as shown below.

two: Measure your box lid against the metal sheet for accuracy. Coat the silver side of the metal with spray adhesive and stick the lid onto it. Fold up the opposing sides with tabs first, followed by the other two sides. Wrap the extra metal over the box edges to finish.

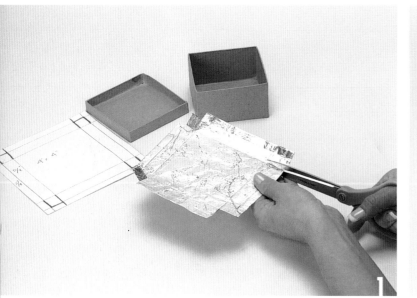

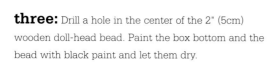

three: Drill a hole in the center of the 2" (5cm) wooden doll-head bead. Paint the box bottom and the bead with black paint and let them dry.

four: Measure the sides of the box and cut enough zebra paper to wrap all the way around the box. Coat the back of the paper with spray adhesive and wrap the paper around the sides of the box.

five: Apply silver spray paint to the four 1½" (4cm) wooden beads and let them dry. Glue the silver beads to each corner of the box bottom for feet. Glue the 2" (5cm) black bead to the center of the box lid as a handle.

•••• finished trinket box

seven: Consider filling your box with fun items such as small pictures, seashells or foreign coins. You know your guests will want to look inside!

woven place mat

Attractive place mats can really liven up a table and add a colorful touch to an otherwise ordi-

nary meal. With the combination of metal and ribbon and traditional weaving techniques,

you'll appreciate these place mats for their incredibly unique design. Use a rotary cutter

instead of scissors to trim the copper strips, and you'll find that this project can be both easy

and fast. Experiment with a variety of ribbon widths, colors and patterns to create a look that

matches your favorite dishes or seasonal decor.

[checklist] • materials & tools

☐ sheet of craft foam   ☐ sheet of copper 8 metal mesh   ☐ textured rubber mallet (See page 12 for instructions on how to make one.)

☐ three sheets of 9¼" x 12" (24cm x 31cm) copper embossing metal   ☐ 14" x 20" (36cm x 51cm) foam core board   ☐ clear quilting ruler

☐ ordinary double-stick tape   ☐ ¼" (6mm) heavy-duty double-stick tape   ☐ 2½ yards (2.25m) of 1" (2.5cm) wire-edged ribbon (in a a color to

match your décor)   ☐ 2 yards (1.8m) of 1½" (4cm) wire-edged ribbon   ☐ fine-point embossing stylus   ☐ rotary cutter   ☐ cutting mat

☐ brayer   ☐ straight pins   ☐ Optional: stain-resistant fabric spray

one: Place the size 8 metal mesh over the foam sheet. One at a time, place the copper metal sheets on top and texture them by hammering with a textured mallet. (See page 13 for basic techniques.) Use a rotary cutter, ruler and cutting mat to cut the metal into fourteen 1" x 12" (2.5cm x 30.5cm) strips and one 1½" x 12" (4cm x 30.5cm) strip. Brayer over each strip to smooth it flat.

two: Create a weaving board by placing strips of ordinary (not heavy-duty) double-stick tape 1" (2.5cm) in from both the top and bottom of the foam core board. Stick the ends of the metal strips to the tape. Start with seven 1" (2.5cm) strips, then the 1½" (4cm) strip, then seven more 1" (2.5cm) strips. The metal strips should bow up from the board, which will make weaving easier.

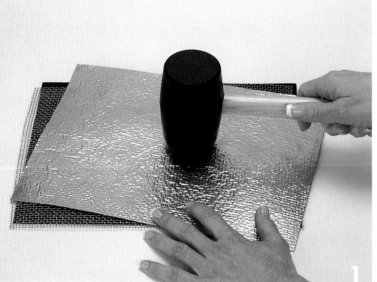

three: Cut five 18" (46cm) lengths of 1½" (4cm) wide ribbon and four 18" (46cm) lengths of 1" (2.5cm) wide ribbon. Starting with the 1" (3cm) wide ribbon, weave through the metal strips. Alternate the widths of ribbon as you continue to weave. Secure the ends with straight pins as you go. When you are finished, remove the pins and place a small piece of heavy-duty double-stick tape between the ribbon and the metal to keep the weaving secure.

four: Remove the place mat from the board. Use a rotary cutter and ruler to trim the place mat to 11¾" x 15¾" (30cm x 40cm).

five: To bind the place mat; cut two 1" x 12" (2.5cm x 30.5cm) strips and four 1" x 9" (2.5cm x 23cm) strips of textured copper metal. Score a fold line lengthwise down the center of each strip. Place heavy-duty double-stick tape lengthwise along the outside edges of each strip and remove the backing. Fold the strips over the edges of the place mat. Brayer over them to secure the bond; trim the corners.

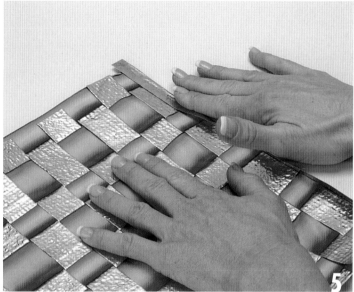

• • • • finished woven place mat

six: You can protect your place mat by spraying it with a water-repellent fabric spray. If you have metal and ribbon left over, you can make matching napkin rings like the one you see here.

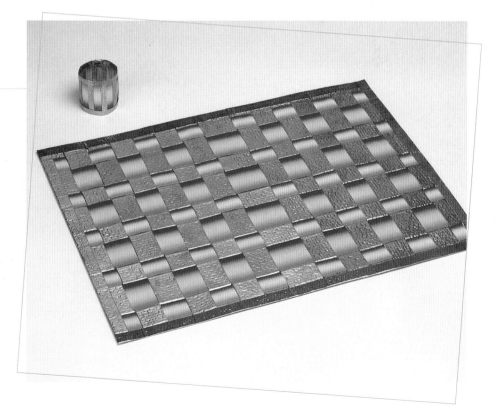

place card holders

When it is time to throw a party, it's the little details that count. Make your guests feel special by displaying their names atop these festive copper place card holders. During the holidays, make them in bright silver and place them on a royal blue or rich red tablecloth to make them stand out. When the celebration is over, your guests can keep them as party favors and use them to display a cherished photo or postcard.

[checklist] • **materials & tools**

☐ 18-gauge plastic-coated copper wire   ☐ short wooden dowel or pencil   ☐ industrial-strength craft glue   ☐ copper hair clips (one per card holder)

☐ foam craft sheet   ☐ sheet of medium-weight copper embossing metal   ☐ card holder templates (page 89)   ☐ textured rubber mallet (See page 12 for instructions on how to make one.)   ☐ 24-gauge copper wire   ☐ 1½" (4cm) wooden doll-head bead   ☐ drill and ⅛" (3mm) drill bit

☐ fine-point embossing stylus   ☐ assorted beads   ☐ copper spray paint   ☐ scissors   ☐ 1/16" (1.5mm) hole punch or awl   ☐ hammer

☐ round-nose pliers   ☐ brayer

one: For each place card holder you plan to make, fold a 12"
(30.5cm) length of wire in half around a dowel. Place the ends of
the wire into the chuck of the drill and tighten to secure. Hold
the dowel in one hand and slowly turn on the drill to twist the
wire together.

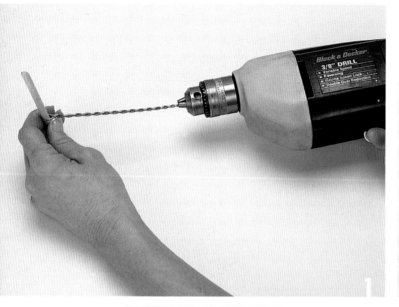

two: Cut the loop off the twisted wire and trim the
rest to 4" (10cm). Glue the wire to a copper hair clip
with industrial-strength craft glue and let it dry.

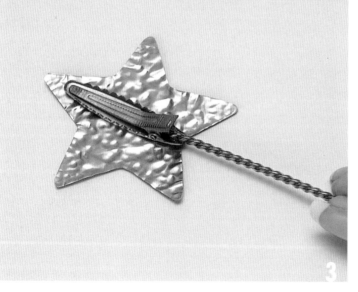

three: Trace one of the four templates onto the copper embossing
metal using a stylus. Cut the star out with scissors, place it on a foam
sheet and texture it with a textured rubber mallet. (See page 13 for basic
techniques.) Brayer over the star to smooth it out. Glue the clip to the
back of the star and let it dry.

four: Punch holes in the bottom points of the star
with a $\frac{1}{16}$" (1.5mm) hole punch or awl. Cut four 1"
(2.5cm) lengths of 24-gauge copper wire. Hammer
the bottom end of each wire down to flatten it and
thread a bead onto each. Trim the top of each wire,
form a loop with round-nose pliers and connect each
of them to the star.

five: Drill a hole into the top of the wooden doll-head bead using a $\frac{1}{8}$" (3mm) bit. Spray it with copper paint and let it dry. Glue the twisted wire in the bead to finish.

finished place card holders

six: Clip name cards into the holders. For even more fun, tuck a photo of each of your guests into the place card holders instead.

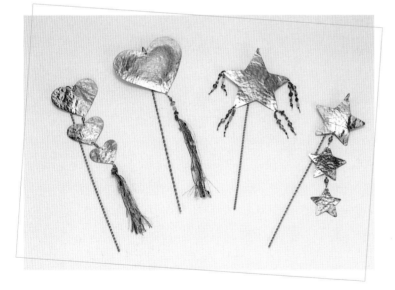

variation: These textured copper hearts and stars also make adorable plant stakes. Heat the edges of each shape with a heat gun and hang them from a stake of twisted wire.

spiral centerpiece

Copper pipe from your local home improvement store may seem like an unlikely decorating

accent, but you're in for a surprise. Spiraled copper tubing makes the perfect surround for this

dramatic mesh vase centerpiece. Fill it with a bold arrangement of silk or dried flowers, or

load it up with bread sticks at your next pasta dinner. Combined with the woven copper place

mats on page 37, this centerpiece will transform any table setting into a work of art.

[checklist] • **materials & tools**

☐ 2½" (6cm) square wooden door-trim rosette   ☐ copper spray paint   ☐ 36" (91cm) of ¼" (6mm) diameter copper tubing   ☐ pipe cutter

☐ industrial-strength craft glue   ☐ sheet of copper 80 mesh   ☐ spiral centerpiece template (page 88)   ☐ ⅛" (3mm) wide heavy-duty

double-stick tape   ☐ drill with ¼" (6mm) drill bit   ☐ wire cutters   ☐ permanent marker   ☐ scissors   ☐ baking sheet   ☐ heat gun

one: Drill a ¼" (6mm) hole in the center of the wood rosette. Spray it with copper paint and let it dry.

two: Cut a 36" (91cm) length of copper tubing. Most hardware stores will cut the copper tubing for you; otherwise, you can use a pipe cutter. Starting 4" (10cm) up from one end, coil the tubing into a cone-shaped spiral. Use a cardboard tube as a guide for making the first wrap of the coil.

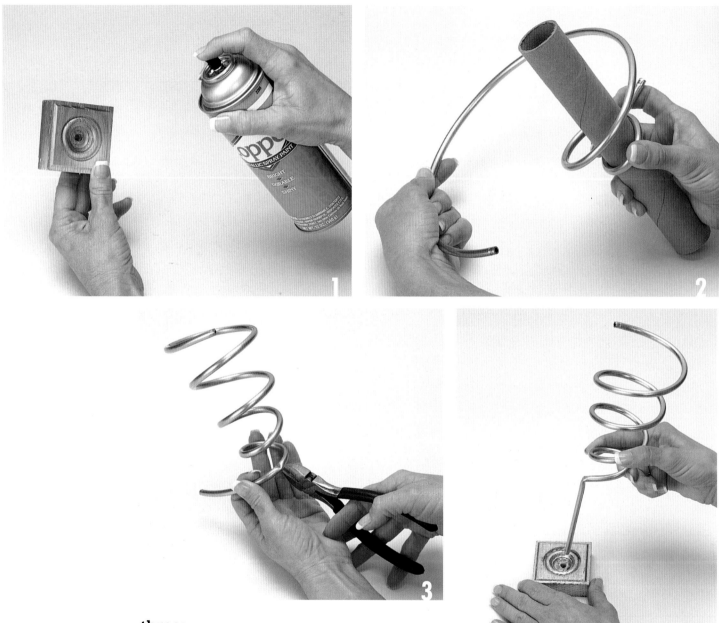

three: Stretch out the coil, if necessary, to achieve the desired shape. Crimp the tube 4" (10cm) from the bottom with wire cutters. Be careful not to cut through the tube.

four: Bend the tube 90° at the crimp. Straighten the tube below the crimp and glue it into the base.

five: Copy the template on page 88. Trace it onto the copper mesh with a permanent marker and cut the shape out. Place the mesh on a baking sheet and use a heat gun to heat along one side and across the top until the edges change color. Let it cool.

six: Place a strip of heavy-duty double-stick tape along the colored side of the mesh. Curl the mesh into a cone shape and secure the ends with the tape.

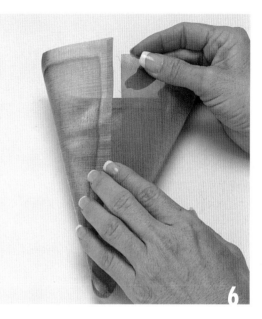

finished spiral centerpiece ● ● ● ●

seven: Finish your centerpiece by placing the cone into the copper-tube surround. You can fill it with fresh flowers if you line the cone with plastic. Or, try placing your centerpiece in a bathroom to hold a hand towel and soap.

✦

lighted garland

Talk about an illuminating decorating idea! This lighted vine garland will make a romantic glowing accent at your next backyard dinner party. Made of several individual elements, once they are bound together they bloom with creative charm. Drape your garland over a patio doorway or hang it among the low branches of a nearby tree. Its twinkling lights, enhanced by the sparkle of the brass leaves and silver vines, add a romantic glow to any space.

[checklist] • materials & tools

□ leaf, flower and vine templates (page 88)   □ 1/8" (3mm) aluminum armature rods, cut into ten 12" (30.5cm) lengths   □ medium-weight brass embossing metal   □ sheet of craft foam   □ 10-light, battery-operated light set   □ sheet of brass 80 metal mesh   □ wire cutters   □ scissors

□ 18-gauge silver plastic-coated wire   □ scalloped edge scissors   □ 1/16" (1.5mm) hole punch   □ permanent marker   □ round-nose pliers

□ fine-point embossing stylus

•••tip | Make embossing easier by placing a sheet of craft foam underneath the metal to cushion it.

two: Trace the leaf template onto the brass metal sheet ten times. Cut out the leaves with scissors. Use a fine-point stylus to emboss the veins in each leaf.

one: Copy the templates on page 88. Cut the aluminum armature rod into ten 12" (30.5cm) lengths. Following the template, bend and spiral each rod using round-nose pliers.

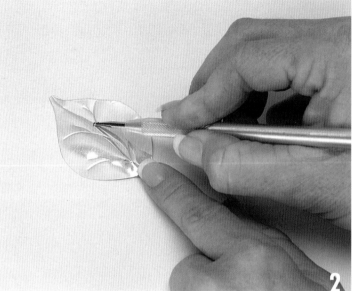

three: Cut ten 12" (30.5cm) lengths of 18-gauge silver plastic-coated wire. Fold each piece of wire in half. Coil the center of the wire around a scrap piece of armature rod, making about five loops.

four: Curl the stems of each of the leaves and slide them into the center of each coil. Crimp the coil with pliers to secure the leaves in place.

five: Attach the leaves to the center of each armature vine by wrapping the silver wire a few times around the armature rod.

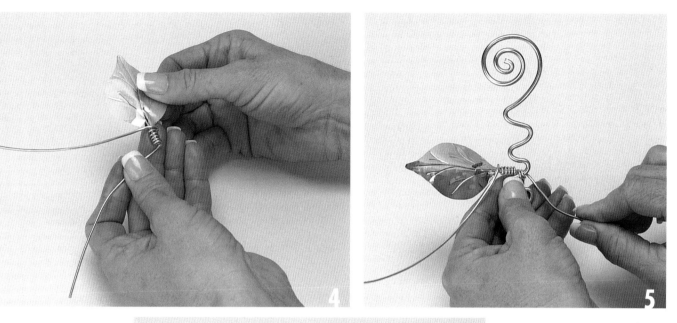

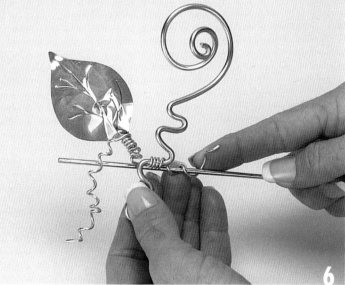

six: Curl the loose ends of the silver wire by coiling them around a scrap piece of armature rod. Continue until you complete all ten leaves and vines.

seven: Cut ten 3" (8cm) squares of brass wire mesh fabric. Fold each square in half and trace the flower pattern on each using a permanent marker. Cut out with scalloped-edge scissors.

eight: Punch a hole in the center of each scallop with a $\frac{1}{16}$" (1.5mm) hole punch to decorate the edge.

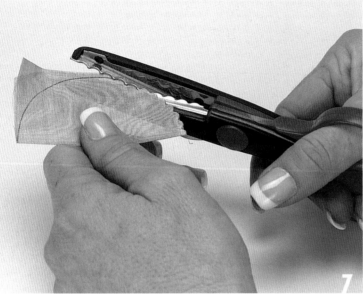

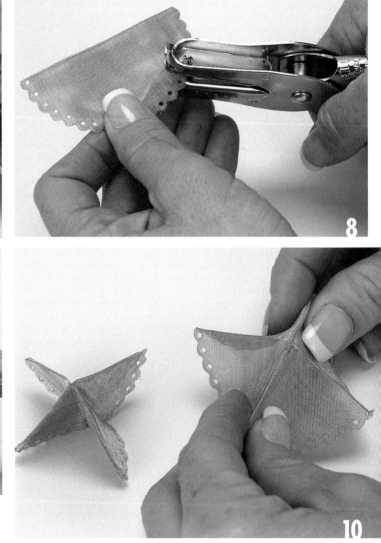

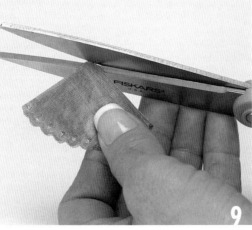

nine: Fold the flower in half again (into quarters) and clip off the tip of the fold.

note: The hole in the center of the flower should be small enough to slide over the lights, yet fit snugly around the light bulb's collar. Experiment on scrap mesh before you try clipping your flowers.

ten: Carefully open each flower and refold it along the pleats as shown above. The pleats should form a cross shape with the scalloped edges cupping toward you.

eleven: Starting with a light bulb centered in the large spiral, attach each vine section by weaving the light cord in and out around the bends in the rod.

twelve: Slide the mesh flowers over each light bulb. After you snuggle the hole in the mesh around the bulb's collar, adjust the flower so that it cups forward.

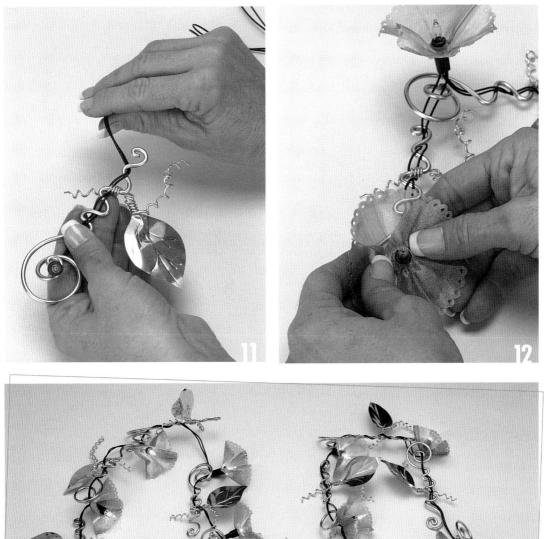

•••• finished lighted garland

thirteen: Whether you use your garland inside or outside, in summer or in winter, it is such a fun way to add a little lighted magic to your surroundings.

⭐

elegant luminaries

Looking for an elegant way to dress up a collection of plain pillar candles? These sleek and striking candle sleeves offer the perfect solution. This project is a perfect marriage of shiny brass wire mesh and brass grommets. Group several luminaries of different heights in and around your garden or entryway to warmly welcome your family and friends with the glow of candlelight. Or how about clustering several together to create an exciting table centerpiece? For a more elaborate effect, weave wire and beads, ribbon, silk flowers, vines, twigs or ivy through the grommet holes of each luminary.

[checklist] • **materials & tools**

□ 8" x 13" (20cm x 33cm) sheet of brass 18 metal mesh   □ 8" x 13" (20cm x 33cm) sheet of paper   □ ¼" (6mm) hole punch

□ ½" (1cm) heavy-duty double-stick tape   □ 18 brass grommets, ¼" (6mm) diameter   □ 6" (15cm) pillar candle   □ scissors

□ ¼" (6mm) grommet setting tool   □ hammer   □ rubber mallet   □ brayer or rolling pin

one: Cut out an 8" x 13" (20cm x 32.5cm) piece of brass mesh and a matching paper template. Create a grid on the template. Measure and mark $\frac{1}{2}$" (1.25cm) in from one side, then continue with 1" (2.5cm) measurements for the rest of the pattern. Punch seven $\frac{1}{4}$" (6mm) holes down each side and thirteen holes across the top of the paper where the lines intersect.

two: Place the paper template over the mesh. Ordinary double-stick tape may be applied to the back of the template to help keep it secure. Using the holes in the template as your guide, punch holes in the mesh.

three: Place a $\frac{1}{4}$" (6mm) grommet onto the base of the setting tool.

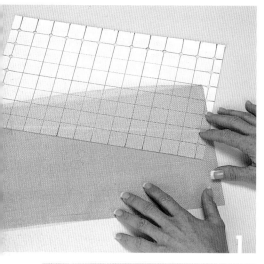

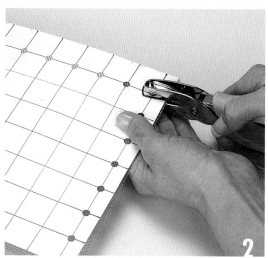

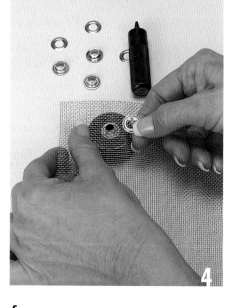

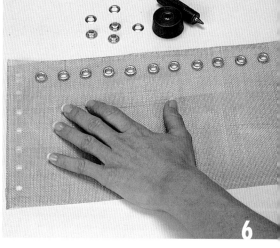

four: Starting with the second hole along the top, place the hole in the mesh over the grommet base and press down firmly. Then place the grommet top over the mesh.

five: Insert the setting tool into the top and hammer to set the grommet into place.

six: Continue setting grommets across the top of the mesh, leaving the first and last holes empty.

seven: Roll the mesh into a tube, overlapping the sides. Align the holes and insert a grommet. This next part is a little tricky, as you have to secure each grommet from inside the tube. Use a rubber mallet to hammer these grommets so you don't mar the mesh.

eight: Use a brayer or rolling pin to smooth out any uneven spots in the mesh.

nine: Create fringe by pulling a few strands of wire from the top of the mesh luminary.

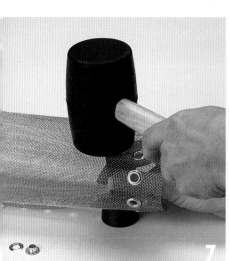
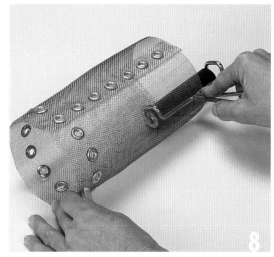
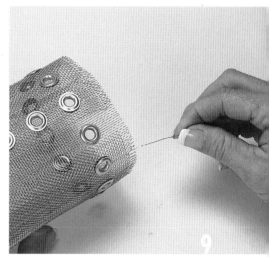

finished mesh luminaries ● ● ● ●

ten: Your luminaries will look fabulous grouped in sets of three. To keep them from tarnishing, spray each luminary with a clear sealant before you place them outside.

perfect pet plant stake

Every garden should be graced with the presence of a favorite pet, and this well-behaved puppy will never trample your tulips. In this project, you'll learn how to add an easy patina finish to embossed brass for a perfectly aged and weathered look. It will look as if your pooch has been guarding the yard for quite some time. Once you try this weathered effect on one project, you'll want to use it on a whole range of matching garden adornments. Finally, if you're a cat lover, don't despair. You'll find a pattern for your favorite feline on page 91!

[checklist] • materials & tools

☐ dog template (page 90)   ☐ 9" x 12" (23cm x 30.5cm) sheet of medium-weight brass embossing metal   ☐ sheet of craft foam   ☐ scissors

☐ patina green antiquing solution   ☐ 18-gauge gold plastic-coated wire   ☐ industrial-strength craft glue   ☐ black acrylic paint   ☐ 30" (76cm)

of ⅛" (3mm) brass armature rod   ☐ fine-point embossing stylus   ☐ contoured embossing tool   ☐ shallow glass dish or bowl   ☐ rubber gloves

☐ round-nose pliers   ☐ ruler   ☐ ⅛" (3mm) hole punch   ☐ needle-nose pliers   ☐ rubber mallet with textured head (See page 12 for

instructions on how to make one.)

one: Enlarge the dog template pieces to the desired size and cut them out. Using a stylus, trace onto the brass sheet one head, one body, one tail and four paws. Be sure to mark all the areas to be embossed. Cut the pieces out and punch holes where indicated on the body and paws.

two: Turn the pieces over onto a foam sheet and retrace the detail lines with a fine-point stylus. Next, using the curved embossing stylus, puff the eyes and nose to achieve depth. Don't worry about following the design exactly. Do what looks good to you.

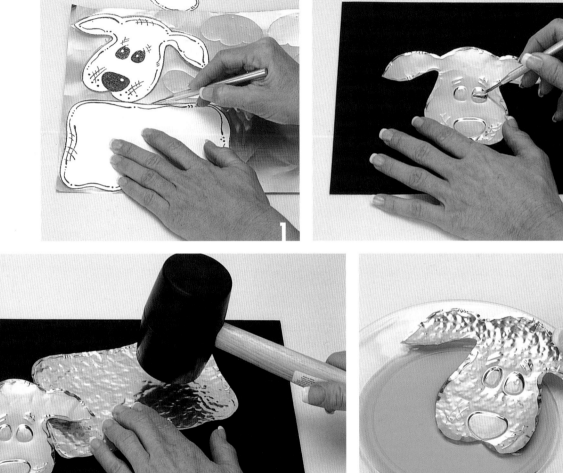

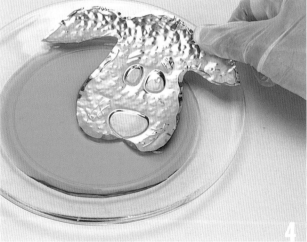

three: Hammer over all the pieces with your textured mallet for added dimension. (See page 13 for basic techniques.)

four: Dip the pieces face down into the patina green antiquing solution for about three minutes. Let dry.

note: Be sure to wear gloves and follow the manufacturer's instructions on the bottle of antiquing solution for tips and safety precautions.

five: Cut four 6" (15cm) lengths of 18-gauge wire and coil them five times around the handle of an embossing tool.

six: Form a closed loop at each end of the first four coils using round-nose pliers. Stretch each of the coils to 3" (8cm).

seven: Create jump rings by cutting through the links of two more coils. You will need eight jump rings.

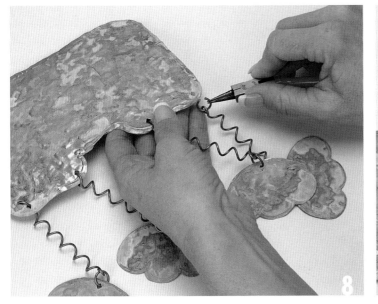

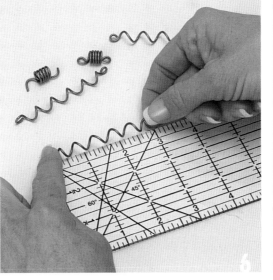

eight: Attach the paws to one end of each coiled wire using the jump rings. Next, attach each of the legs to the body the same way.

nine: Cut a 1" x 6" (2.5cm x 15cm) strip of scrap metal. Form it into a loop and glue it to the body where the head will go. This will give your dog added dimension.

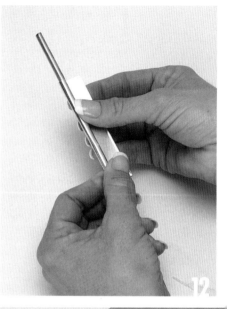

ten: Position and glue the head onto the metal loop. Glue the tail into place. While the glue is still wet, angle the head and tail into desired position. Let dry.

eleven: Dab a bit of black acrylic paint onto the eyes and nose.

twelve: To create the holder for the plant stake, cut a 1" x 3" (2.5cm x 8cm) strip of scrap metal. Roll it lengthwise around the armature rod, creating a tube.

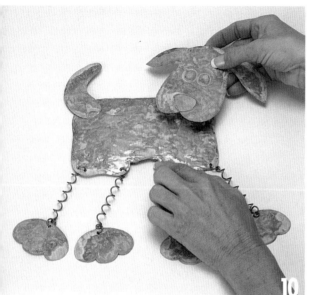

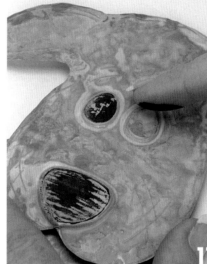

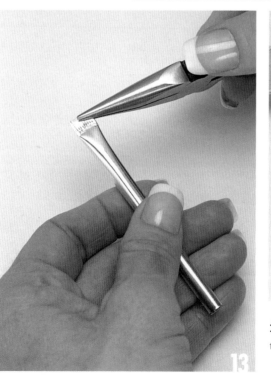

thirteen: Crimp one end of the tube with needle-nose pliers to close it.

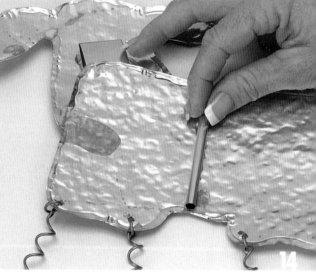

fourteen: Glue the tube to the back of the dog. Let it dry, then slide the armature rod into the tube.

fifteen: Select a choice location in your garden and sink the armature rod into the soil, making sure it's secure before placing the dog onto the rod.

●●● • **variation:** If you are fond of cats, you'll find the template for this kitty on page 91.

beaded flower pot

Your common houseplant will look extraordinary once it's planted in this one-of-a-kind clay pot. You can dress up any pot with this scalloped pewter band that has been textured, antiqued and embellished with colorful bead fringe. For a more dramatic effect, trim pots of different sizes and group them together on a garden wall or a patio table for a wonderful centerpiece. This technique can also be used to add a decorative trim to a plain wooden shelf.

[checklist] • **materials & tools**

☐ wavy-edge stencil ☐ sheet of medium-weight pewter embossing metal ☐ sheet of craft foam ☐ sheet of 8 metal mesh ☐ soft cloth or paper towel ☐ olive-gold and emerald Rub 'n Buff ☐ 4" (10cm) clay pot ☐ black nylon beading thread ☐ assorted beads ☐ ¼" (6mm) heavy-duty double-stick tape ☐ fine-point embossing stylus ☐ scissors ☐ textured rubber mallet (See page 12 for instructions on how to make one.) ☐ brayer ☐ ¹⁄₁₆" (1.5mm) hole punch ☐ plastic gloves ☐ needle tool or T-pin ☐ Optional: 1.5mm crochet hook

one: Cut a strip of pewter metal to 1½" x 12" (4cm x 31cm). Using the stencil as your guide, trace a wavy line along one side of the pewter strip with a fine-point stylus.

two: Cut out the wavy edge with scissors. Place the mesh screen over the foam sheet and texture the pewter using the textured rubber mallet. Brayer over the pewter to smooth it out.

three: Punch holes in the center of each scallop with a ¹⁄₁₆" (1.5mm) hole punch. Apply a mixture of the green and olive Rub 'n Buff with a soft cloth. Let dry for three minutes, then buff with a clean cloth.

four: Apply Rub 'n Buff to the clay pot, including the top of the rim. Allow some of the pot to show through the paint for a soft, weathered look.

●●● **tip** If your thread is not stiff enough to pick up beads, use a beading needle and longer thread.

five: Cut the beading thread into several 8" (20cm) lengths. Fold each thread in half and use a crochet hook, if necessary, to insert the looped thread through the holes in the pewter strip. Pull the ends of the thread through the loop to secure. String on assorted beads and use a needle tool to help snug a knot against the beads.

six: Attach the finished trim to the pot with heavy-duty double-stick tape. Cut off any excess trim.

finished flower pot ● ● ● ●

seven: Your pot is now ready for one of your favorite plants. If you don't have a green thumb, you can fill your trimmed pot with a silk ivy topiary or a bouquet of dried lavender.

✪

dragonfly plant stake

A creature as elusive as a dragonfly can be enjoyed year-round when you make your own.

Here, the combination of wire, metal and beads adds a special touch to this delicate creature.

Our dragonfly is the perfect size to embellish a potted plant. When the wind is just right, the

spring holding him aloft will cause his wings to flutter and catch your eye with their sparkle.

And, in case you're inspired to plant a larger dragonfly in your garden, there are tips on how

to make one on page 73. It uses the same basic techniques as this tiny one, but it has its own

unique look.

[checklist] • materials & tools

□ dragonfly wing template (page 89)   □ sheet of medium-weight aluminum embossing metal   □ 18-gauge silver plastic-coated wire

□ 6" (15cm) of ⅛" (3mm) silver aluminum armature rod   □ 24-gauge silver wire   □ ⅛" (3mm) silver eyelet   □ one 8mm bead

□ seed beads in assorted colors   □ wooden dowel   □ fine-point embossing stylus   □ needle tool or T-pin   □ foam craft sheet

□ scissors   □ round-nose pliers   □ industrial-strength craft glue   □ drill

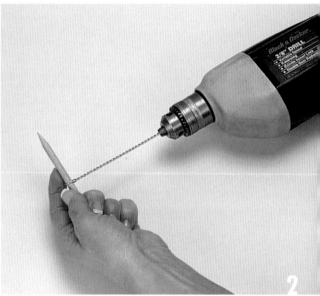

one: Cut a 2" x 5" (5cm x 13cm) piece of aluminum embossing metal and place it on a foam sheet. Trace the wing template from page 89 onto the metal. Emboss the details with a fine-point stylus. Using the template as your guide, punch holes around the edges of the wings with a needle tool and cut the wings out.

two: Cut 12" (31cm) of 18-gauge wire. Fold it in half around a wooden dowel. Place the loose ends of the wire into the drill chuck; tighten to secure. While holding the dowel in one hand, slowly turn on the drill with the other hand to twist the wires together. Trim the twisted wire to 4" (10cm), leaving the loop. This will become the dragonfly's head.

•••tip

Instead of using a needle tool to punch holes around the wing edges, you can also use a sewing pattern tracing wheel for an embossed effect.

four: Wrap the remaining wire and beads back toward the head. Secure the wire with another tight wrap under the head, leaving a wire tail. Trim off the looped ends. Slide the 8mm bead onto both wires.

three: String 5" (13cm) of seed beads onto 16" (41cm) of 24-gauge wire. Make a small loop at the ends to keep the beads from sliding off. Starting just under the head, leave a 1½" (4cm) wire tail, make one tight wrap to secure the wire, then loosely loop the beaded wire down 1½" to 2" (4cm to 5cm) around the body, spreading beads out as you go.

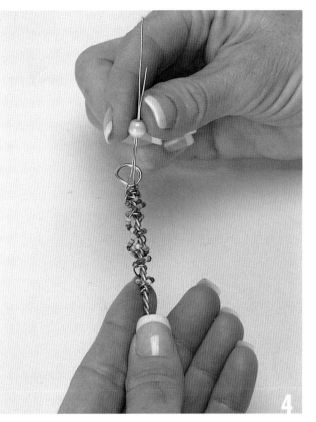

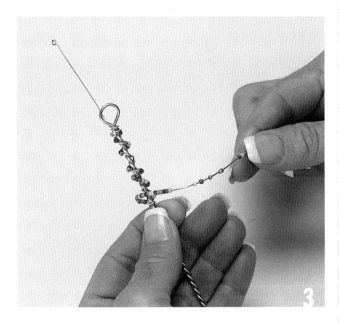

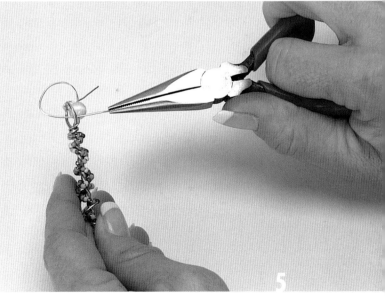

five: Wrap each wire around the top of the loop to secure the bead. Trim the wires to an even length.

six: Curl ends of each wire with round-nose pliers to form the antennae. Glue the body onto the center portion of the wings. Let it dry.

seven: Turn the dragonfly over and glue a ⅛" (3mm) eyelet onto the center of the body. Coil 4" (10cm) of 24-gauge wire around the 6"(15cm) piece of ⅛" (3mm) armature rod to form a spring. Glue the spring around the eyelet and let it dry.

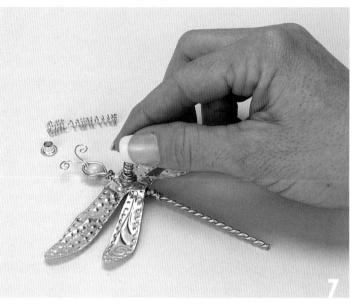

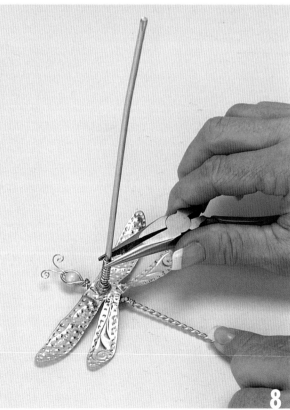

eight: Place the armature rod in the end of the spring and crimp the end with needle-nose pliers to secure the rod.

nine: Place your finished dragonfly into any potted plant indoors or out.

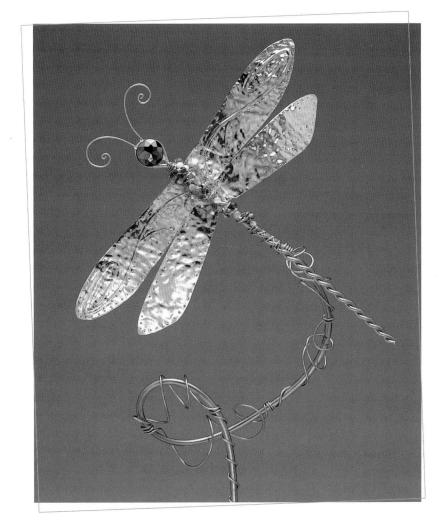

● ● ● **variation:** To make this larger version, enlarge the wing template on page 89 for 9" (23cm) wings and transfer it to medium-weight brass embossing metal. Twist 20" (51cm) of ⅛" (3mm) aluminum armature wire to form the body and trim to 8½" (22cm). Wrap and form antennae with 25" (63cm) of 18-gauge silver plastic-coated wire strung with 30 beads. Glue on a large jewel head and mount the tube to a ⅜" (5mm) armature rod by using the same mount as the dog stake on page 62.

whimsical plant jewelry

What a perfect way to add a little whimsy to a favorite potted plant. This charming bit of "plant jewelry" is an ideal excuse to use up your leftover beads, wire and scrap embossing metal. You can make one of these decorations in less than an hour and tuck it into a small plant to cheer up someone you care about or spread a little joy among friends. Experiment with the free-form pattern of bends, loops and spirals so that no two turn out exactly alike.

[checklist] • materials & tools

☐ heart template (page 92) ☐ 2" x 2" (5cm x 5cm) square piece of medium-weight aluminum embossing metal ☐ 12" (31cm) of 18-gauge silver plastic-coated wire ☐ 12" (31cm) of ⅛" (3mm) silver aluminum armature rod ☐ 24-gauge silver wire ☐ olive-gold and emerald Rub 'n Buff ☐ soft cloth or paper towel ☐ assorted seed beads ☐ silver jump ring ☐ fine-point and contour embossing styluses ☐ needle tool or T-pin ☐ foam craft sheet ☐ scissors ☐ round-nose pliers ☐ ¹⁄₁₆" (1.5mm) hole punch

one: Cut a 2" x 2" (5cm x 5cm) piece of aluminum metal and place it on a foam sheet. Trace the heart template and details with a fine-point stylus. Puff the heart out with a contour stylus. Add texture to the center by tapping with the fine-point stylus. Punch holes around the edges with a needle tool.

two: Cut the heart out and punch a hole at the top and bottom of the heart with a ¹⁄₁₆" (1.5m) hole punch or needle tool. Apply a mixture of the emerald and olive-green Rub 'n Buff with a cloth. Let dry three minutes and buff with a clean cloth.

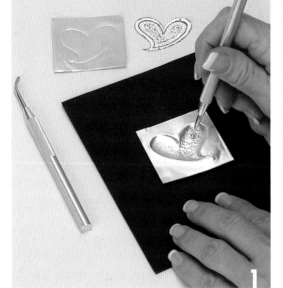

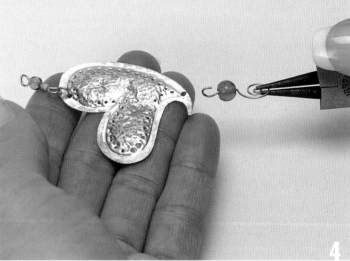

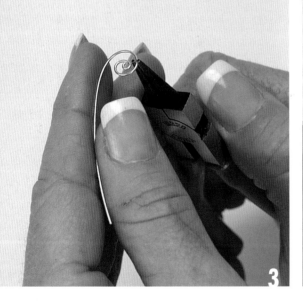

three: Cut 2" (5cm) of 24-gauge wire and make a spiral at one end with round-nose pliers.

four: Add a bead to the spiraled wire, trimming the wire if necessary. Form a loop at the other end and attach it to the bottom of the heart. Cut 1" (2.5cm) of 24-gauge wire; form a loop at one end and add a few beads. Trim the end if necessary; form another loop and attach to the top of the heart with a jump ring.

five: Cut 34" (86cm) of 18-gauge wire. Starting at the center of the wire, wrap each end three or four times around the end of the armature rod. Free form the remaining wire into bends and loops. Round-nose pliers and the end of a stylus will help in this creative process. Use the photo above as your guide or just design as you go. Finish each end with a spiral.

six: String about 6" (15cm) of seed beads onto 36" (91cm) of 24-gauge wire. Starting at one end, make a few tight wraps to secure the beaded wire around the heavier free-formed wire. Then start creating little beaded curves and loops. Finish each loop or two with a few tight wraps and trim. Continue across to other side.

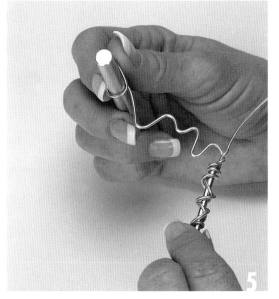

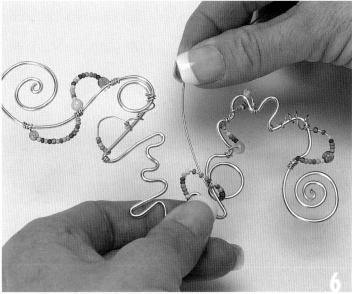

tip

Make a small loop at the ends of the wire to keep beads from sliding off.

•••• finished plant jewelry

seven: Attach the heart charm at the bottom of the spiral. For an interesting variation, try using different colored beads or metals and dangle an embossed star or moon from the spiral.

glowing blossoms

Art and nature come together in these magnificent garden torches. These elaborate copper blooms will dazzle at any time of the day, reflecting both sunlight and candlelight with a warm glow. They are sure to become your favorite decoration at cookouts and lazy summer garden parties. In the winter, mount a few torches on the floor among several tall potted plants for a dramatic indoor arrangement. Plant a few in your yard this weekend. Best of all, they don't require any weeding or watering to be enjoyed!

[checklist] • materials & tools

☐ flower petal templates (page 92)   ☐ three sheets of medium-weight copper embossing metal   ☐ ½" (1cm) wide heavy-duty double-stick tape ☐ ½" (1cm) diameter copper pipe (for three blossoms, cut the pipe to 3 ft. [90cm], 3½ ft. [105cm] and 4 ft. [120cm]). Most hardware stores will cut the pipe for you.   ☐ 1" x ½" (2.5cm x 1.5cm) pipe reducer/connector fitting   ☐ 3½" (9cm) diameter steel floor flange   ☐ copper spray paint   ☐ ½" (1.5cm) diameter threaded pipe fitting   ☐ industrial-strength craft glue   ☐ 24-gauge copper wire   ☐ small glass hurricane lamp with a ½" (1.5cm) rubber base   ☐ tea light candle   ☐ fine-point embossing stylus   ☐ textured rubber mallet (See page 12 for instructions on how to make one.)   ☐ sheet of craft foam   ☐ scissors   ☐ baking sheet   ☐ heat gun   ☐ rotary cutter   ☐ cutting mat   ☐ ruler

☐ Optional: needle-nose pliers

one: Copy the leaf templates and cut them out. Place the copper on a foam sheet and trace seven large petals and five small petals. Emboss the veins in each petal with a fine-point stylus. Two large petals will become leaves.

two: Texture the copper leaves by placing the metal on the foam sheet and hitting it with the textured rubber mallet.

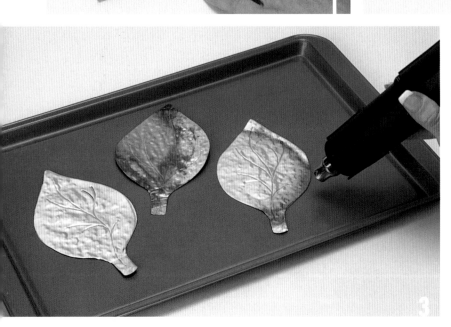

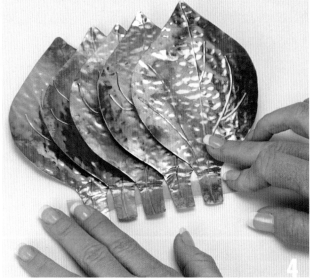

three: Cut out the leaves with scissors. Place the petals on a baking sheet and heat them with a heat gun until the edges change color.

four: Cut a 5" (13cm) strip of heavy-duty double-stick tape. Leave the backing on and place the tape sticky side up. Place a row of five petals along the tape, attaching the stems to the tape ¼" (6mm) apart.

five: Stick another 5" (13cm) strip of double-stick tape over the stems of the large petals. Remove the backing and adhere the five small petals between the large ones, with the last small petal on the outside.

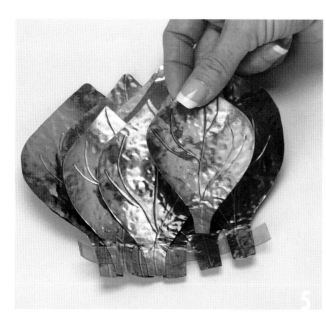

●●● **tip**

If you find it easier, you can also glue the petals into the fitting.

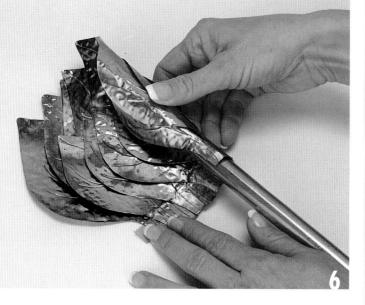

six: Roll the petals around the end of the copper pipe to form a cone shape.

seven: Remove the backing from the first layer of tape and stick the rolled petals into the wide end of the connector pipe fitting.

eight: On a cutting mat, use a rotary cutter to cut a 2¼" x 9" (6cm x 23cm) piece of copper. Measure and cut nine ¼" (6mm) strips, stopping 1" (2.5cm) short of the top.

nine: Spiral each piece of fringe around a rod or twist each of the ¼" (6mm) strips by hand.

ten: Place the fringe on a baking sheet and heat it with a heat gun to change the color.

eleven: Roll the fringe into a tube slightly smaller than the ½"(1.5cm) tube made with the petals. Wrap a strip of double-stick tape around the base; remove the backing and insert the fringe down into the center of the petals.

twelve: Spray the steel floor flange with copper paint. Screw the threaded copper fitting into the floor flange, using pliers if necessary. This forms the base for the blossom.

thirteen: Insert the copper pipe into the base. Attach the leaves to the pipe by wrapping copper wire around the stem portion of the leaf. Add a dab of glue for added security.

finished glowing blossom • • • •

fifteen: Insert the glass hurricane lamp into the center of the blossom and add a tea light candle. Arrange the fringe around the hurricane for the finishing touch. Enjoy the sunlight reflecting off the copper petals during the day; light the candles and enjoy the orange glow after dark.

fourteen: Open and arrange the petals of the blossom. Petals can be bent and crimped for a more natural look.

✦

winged ladybug

Now you can bring one of the gardener's most valuable creatures to your very own garden.

Let this adorable ladybug mingle among your spring flowers or greet guests at your front step.

She offers the best of everything in a metalcraft project: a mix of copper metal and mesh and

a combination of my favorite embossing and heating techniques. Better yet, the feet are

made out of recycled bottle caps that are spray painted to match.

[checklist] • materials & tools

☐ ladybug template (page 93)   ☐ sheet of medium-weight copper embossing metal   ☐ sheet of craft foam   ☐ sheet of copper 80 metal mesh

☐ 18-gauge copper plastic-coated wire   ☐ six bottle caps   ☐ two clear glass gems   ☐ fine-point embossing stylus   ☐ permanent marker

☐ scrap of brass or gold aluminum embossing metal (for use in the eyes)   ☐ scissors   ☐ baking sheet   ☐ heat gun   ☐ copper spray paint

☐ awl or nail   ☐ hammer   ☐ ¹⁄₁₆" (1.5mm) hole punch   ☐ round-nose pliers   ☐ industrial-strength craft glue   ☐ Optional: clear sealant

one: Trace and cut out the ladybug template. Trace the body template and embossing details on the copper metal with a fine-point stylus; be sure to mark the hole placement for the legs. Trace the wing template on the copper wire mesh fabric with a permanent marker. Cut out the wings.

two: Place the metal on a sheet of foam and use the stylus to add definition to all the embossing details (nose, mouth, back). Cut out and punch holes for the legs with a $\frac{1}{16}$" (1.5mm) hole punch.

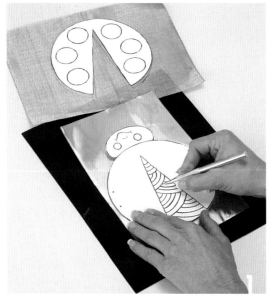

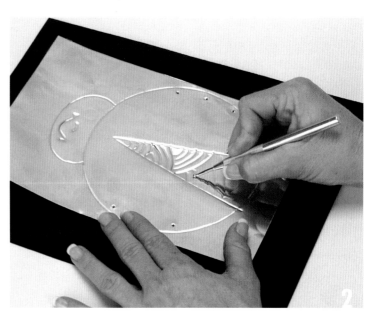

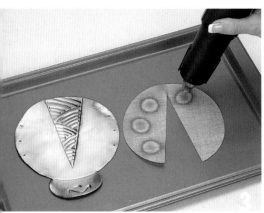

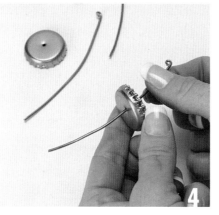

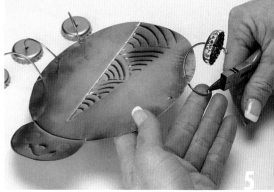

three: Place the body and wings on a baking sheet. Heat the body with a heat gun to change its colors. Heat the wings using the spot technique (see page 14) to create colored dots.

four: Punch a hole in the center of six bottle caps with an awl or nail and hammer. Spray the caps with copper paint. Cut six 4" (10cm) lengths of copper wire; form a small loop at one end. Slide a wire through the hole in each bottle cap.

five: Curve each wire leg to form an arch. Thread each leg through the top of the holes on the body. Use round-nose pliers to form a loop in the end of each wire to secure it.

six: Cut 6" (15cm) of copper wire for the antennae and form a spiral on each end with pliers. Apply a bead of industrial-strength glue at the base of the head and sandwich the antennae between the wings and the body.

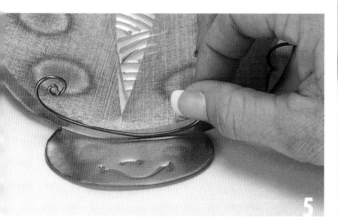

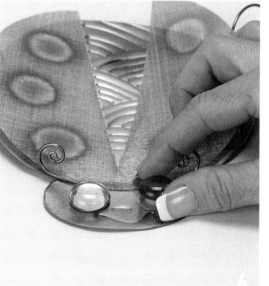

seven: Cut two ½" (1.5cm) circles of brass or gold aluminum metal for the eyes. Glue them into place, then glue the clear glass gems over the eyes. Let the eyes dry.

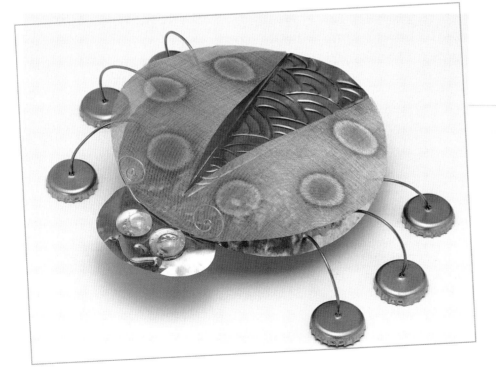

finished ladybug ••••

eight: Prop your ladybug up on an overturned clay pot in a favorite spot in your garden. To keep the copper shiny, spray it with a coat of clear sealant before placing it outdoors.

Project Templates

●●●● The following templates can be used to complete the projects in this book. All the templates are shown full size except where otherwise noted. To reproduce any of these templates, make a photocopy or trace over the template with tracing paper. Press down with a stylus to transfer the pattern onto metal foil. To transfer the pattern onto wire mesh, draw around the cut-out pattern with a permanent marker.

●●● This template is for the Spiral Centerpiece on page 45. You need to enlarge this template 182%. At full size, it should look like an 8¼" (21cm) square with one corner cut off. Use a permanent marker to trace it on mesh.

●●● These three templates are for the Lighted Garland on page 49.

••• These four templates
are for the Place Card
Holders on page 41.

••• This template is for the Dragonfly Plant Stake
on page 69. To make the larger dragonfly
shown on page 73, enlarge the pattern by
194% on a photocopier.

●●● This template is for the Perfect Pet Plant Stake on page
59. The spots marked with an "X" show where to punch
a hole in the metal foil. Use a photocopier and enlarge
this template 111%.

●●● This template is for the
Perfect Cat Stake on page
63. The spots marked with
an "X" show where to
punch a hole in the metal
foil. Use a photocopier
and enlarge this template
111%.

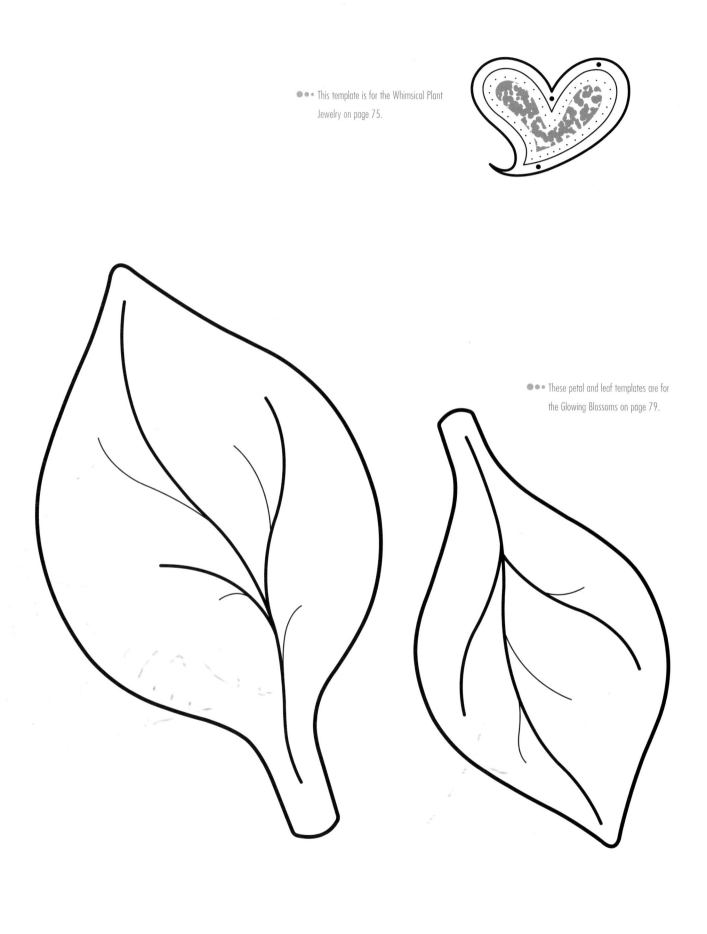

●●● This template is for the Whimsical Plant
Jewelry on page 75.

●●● These petal and leaf templates are for
the Glowing Blossoms on page 79.

These templates are for the Winged
Ladybug on page 85. Use a photocopier
and enlarge these templates 111%.

Resources

Most of the tools and supplies used in this book are readily available at your local craft and home improvement stores. You may also find materials by contacting the suppliers listed below. Check their Web sites for the store location nearest you.

Suppliers in the US

Home Depot
(770) 433-8211
www.homedepot.com
☐ general hardware store

Michaels Stores, Inc.
(800) MICHAELS
www.michaels.com
☐ general craft stores—Central US

Hobby Lobby
(405) 745-1100
www.hobbylobby.com
☐ general craft stores—Central US

AC Moore
www.acmoore.com
☐ general craft stores—Eastern US

Paramount Wire Co.
CBC Metal Supply
2-8 Central Ave.
East Orange, NJ 07018
(973) 672-0500
wirestore@parawire.com
www.parawire.com
☐ craft wire and tools

Suppliers in Canada

MacPherson Craft Supplies
(519) 284-1741
www.macphersoncrafts.com
☐ general craft stores

Home Depot
1-800-668-2266
www.homedepot.com
☐ general hardware store

Revy Home & Garden Home Centers
Western Canada: (604) 882-6200
Eastern Canada: (416) 241-8844
www.revy.com

Suppliers in the U.K.

Beadworks/JRM Beads, Ltd.
16 Redbridge Enterprise Centre Thompson Close
Ilford, Essex IG1 1TY
(020) 8553 3240
tah@beadworks.co.uk
www.beadworks.com
☐ beads, wire and tools

Art Emboss
Call (020) 8888 6888 for details of your nearest stockist.
☐ embossing metal and mesh

C.A.T.S. Group
PO Box 12
Saxmundham, IP17 3NT
+44 (1)728 648717
Fax: +44 (1)728 648593
info@catsgroup.co.uk
www.catsgroup.co.uk
☐ embossing metal and mesh

Product Manufacturers

American Art Clay Co., Inc.
4717 16th Street
Indianapolis, IN 46222
(800) 374-1600
catalog@amaco.com
www.amaco.com
☐ embossing metal and mesh

Artistic Wire Ltd.
752 N. Larch Avenue
Elmhurst, IL 60126
(630) 530-7567
artwire97@aol.com
www.artisticwire.com
☐ craft wire

Fiskars
7811 W. Stewart Ave.
Wausau, WI 54401
(715) 842-2091
www.fiskars.com
☐ scissors and cutting tools

Krylon
101 Prospect Ave. NW 15 Midland
Cleveland, OH 44115
(216) 515-7693
www.krylon.com
☐ metallic spray paints

Modern Options
1930 Fairway Dr.
San Leandro, CA 94577
(510) 895-8000
info@modernoptions.com
www.modernoptions.com
☐ metal patinas

ScottiCrafts, Division of TSI
460 E. Sandford Blvd.
Mount Vernon, NY 10550
(914) 668-3700
info@scotticrafts.com
www.scotticrafts.com
☐ Ultimate Bond tape

Uchida of America Corp
3535 Del Amo Blvd
Torrance, CA 90503
(310) 869-6388
www.uchida.com
☐ cutting mats, heat guns and embossing tools

Zucker Feather Products
512 N. East Street
California, MO 65018
(573) 796-2183
zfeathers@aol.com
www.zuckerfeathers.com
☐ cutting mats, heat guns and embossing tools

Index

give your **home & garden** a personal touch with style!

Try any of these **twenty decorative mosaic projects!** Each one includes step-by-step instructions, materials lists and templates you can enlarge and trace. There's no tile to cut and no messy grout. Just pick a project and get creative! From garden stepping stones to table tops, you'll find beautiful mosaic projects for every part of your home.

ISBN 1-58180-129-7, paperback, 128 pages, #31830-K

Use polymer clay to create **elegant decor for your home!** Nineteen step-by-step projects make getting started easy. You'll learn how to combine clay with fabric, silverware and other household items, plus metallic powders that simulate colored glass, antique bronze or gleaming silver. You'll also find instructions for color mixing, marbling and caning.

ISBN 1-58180-139-4, paperback, 128 pages, #31880-K

You can make **your own tabletop fountains** and add beautiful accents to your living room, bedroom, kitchen and garden. These 15 gorgeous step-by-step projects make it easy, using everything from lava rock and bamboo to shells and clay pots. You'll learn to incorporate flowers, driftwood, fire, figurines, crystals, plants and more.

ISBN 1-58180-103-3, paperback, 128 pages, #31791-K

Create **rustic, whimsical houses** perfect for use indoors and out. Lucinda Macy provides step-by-step instructions and full-color photos that make every project easy. There are 13 designs in all, including birdhouses, decorative fairy and gnome homes, and garden homes for toads. Each one can be embellished with acorns, moss, seedpods, twigs and other natural materials.

ISBN 1-58180-071-1, paperback, 128 pages, #31793-K

These books and other fine **North Light** titles are available from your local art & craft retailer, bookstore, online supplier or by calling **1-800-448-0915.**